STRENGTH

for the

BATTLE

Declarations for Putting on the Whole Armour of God

REVEREND MICHAEL O. BALOGUN

authorHOUSE®

AuthorHouse™ UK
1663 Liberty Drive
Bloomington, IN 47403 USA
www.authorhouse.co.uk
Phone: UK TFN: 0800 0148641 (Toll Free inside the UK)
        UK Local: 02036 956322 (+44 20 3695 6322 from outside the UK)

Published by AuthorHouse 11/24/2020

ISBN: 978-1-6655-8272-8 (sc)
ISBN: 978-1-6655-8273-5 (hc)
ISBN: 978-1-6655-8271-1 (e)

Print information available on the last page.

This book is printed on acid-free paper.

Scripture taken from the King James Version of the Bible.

This book is dedicated to the Godhead: the Father, the Son, and the Holy Spirit for the revelation of the armour of God, enabling my family and me to stand and be victorious during several periods of spiritual warfare.

To the ministers and ministries that gave me the opportunity to preach about the armour of God over the years.

To all those who have encouraged me by their testimonies of victory through what they have learned about how to put on the armour as described in this book.

To all those who are facing spiritual battles and desire to know how to be victorious, and how not to be a casualty in spiritual warfare.

CONTENTS

ACKNOWLEDGEMENTS

Blessed be the name of the Lord for the revelation on how to put on the whole armour of God.

I feel a deep sense of gratitude and appreciation to my wife and children for reviewing the book and for their encouragement and prayers.

I thank my brothers and my friends for their encouragement.

I am also grateful to all, too numerous to mention, the Lord used to teach, mentor, and counsel me in ministry.

Finally, I thank all the ministries and churches who opened their doors for me to minister in spiritual warfare.

INTRODUCTION

As a young believer, after my discipleship training, I was part of the deliverance team of the Christian fellowship where I was growing spiritually. We ministered deliverance to many Christian believers. As I matured as a Christian and started to minister the gospel of the kingdom, I witnessed Christians being attacked with mental illness, Christians being threatened by unbelievers with resultant fear, Christian families breaking down, increased fornication and adultery, envy, jealousy, and so on. We were taught that we were more than conquerors.

I was concerned about this and started to pray to the Lord to show me how I could be so strong that the enemy would be unable to destroy me. I started studying but couldn't find many books teaching about this. The ones I found said that there was no protection for the back. Others said that once you are walking in holiness, you are automatically protected. Others taught that there was only one weapon of offence, and the others are for defence. I couldn't agree with any of these teachings.

How can God give us incomplete armour? If it is the whole armour of God, then it has to be a perfect and complete armour, offering total and perfect protection for the Christian who is born again.

If we are commanded to put on the whole armour of God, how then can it be on us automatically? God revealed to me that He gave us a perfect and complete armour for total protection and that we should put on the armour of God daily. He revealed that we have more than one piece of the armour for offence, and the pieces of the armour work together in an interrelated manner and function. These teachings are revealed in this book.

Jesus Christ blotted out; that is, He totally wiped out the handwriting of ordinances, the record of all the charges against us. He took it out of the way by nailing it to the cross. He spoiled (disarmed) principalities and powers, making a public show of them, demonstrating to the entire universe and the unseen realms His total victory as Lord of lords and King of kings.

Jesus took over the keys of hell and death so that anyone who has accepted Him as Lord and Saviour is no longer under the jurisdiction and authority of Satan. Jesus now has the keys of hell and death in His hands.

It is now our responsibility to enforce Calvary's victory and Satan's defeat. We have the victory (1 Corinthians 15:57). The devil is now destroyed; he has been made powerless, brought to nought, and paralysed as far as believers are concerned. Put on the armour daily, and you will not be a casualty of the enemy.

I have received many wonderful testimonies from believers who have been practising the principles in this book.

This book teaches practical ways of putting on the armour and the declarations of scriptures that guarantee your victory.

My prayer is that the Lord will grant you understanding as you read this book in Jesus name. Amen.

CHAPTER 1

BE STRONG

In spite of the bad news we hear about the turmoil and upheavals around us—pestilences, disasters, floods, earthquakes, wars and rumours of war, economic challenges, and breakdowns of law and order—God does not want us to fall apart or become overwhelmed.

In I Corinthians 16:13 He commands believers to be strong:

Watch ye, stand fast in the faith, quit you like men, be strong.

This scripture simply means that we should be vigilant, on guard, and not be fearful but courageous and strong in all our actions.

In Ephesians 6:10–18 we are commanded to be strong in the Lord and in the power of His might:

> Finally, my brethren, be strong in the Lord, and in
> the power of his might.

Put on the whole armour of God, that ye may be able to stand against the wiles of the devil.

For we wrestle not against flesh and blood, but against principalities, against powers, against the rulers of the darkness of this world, against spiritual wickedness in high places.

Wherefore take unto you the whole armour of God, that ye may be able to withstand in the evil day, and having done all, to stand.

Stand therefore, having your loins girt about with truth, and having on the breastplate of righteousness;

And your feet shod with the preparation of the gospel of peace;

Above all, taking the shield of faith, wherewith ye shall be able to quench all the fiery darts of the wicked.

And take the helmet of salvation, and the sword of the Spirit, which is the word of God:

Praying always with all prayer and supplication in the Spirit, and watching thereunto with all perseverance and supplication for all saints.

We need to be strong in the Lord and in the power of His might if we are to accomplish God's assignments and fulfil our purposes and destinies.

In Joshua 1:9, God commanded Joshua to be strong:

> Have not I commanded thee? Be strong and of a good courage; be not afraid, neither be thou dismayed: for the Lord thy God is with thee withersoever thou goest.

Joshua and the people of Israel were making preparations to go into battle in order to defeat the nations of Canaan and their commander. The Lord and Commander of the armies of heaven ordered Joshua to be strong.

We need strength for the battles that all believers have to face in their journeys in this world, as Ephesians 6:10 makes clear:

Finally, my brethren, be strong in the Lord, and in the power of his might.

THE BATTLE WE FIGHT: GOD IS OUR STRENGTH

Many scriptures in the Bible reveal to us that the Lord is our strength, the source of our strength, and that He is the one who gives us victory in any battle we face (Psalms 18:1–2, 32, 39; 27:1–3; 28:7; 29:11; 46:1; 1 Corinthians 15:57; 2 Corinthians 2:14; Romans 8:37; Isaiah 45:24).

Psalm 27:1 declares that God is the source of strength for His people.

> The Lord is my light and my salvation; whom shall I fear? The Lord is the strength of my life; of whom shall I be afraid?

Psalm 18:32 and 39 declare that God is the one who arms us with strength for the battle.

> It is God that girdeth me with strength, and maketh my way perfect.

> For thou hast girded me with strength unto the battle: thou hast subdued under me those that rose up against me.

Philippians 4:13 reveals this truth:

> I can do all things through Christ which strengtheneth me.

Brethren, we can do all things through the Lord Jesus Christ who strengthens us. The strength you need to fulfil your purpose or the assignment you have at present is available through Christ.

Jesus Christ, our Lord and Saviour, defeated the devil through His death on the cross and His resurrection on the third day. Jesus has completely won the battle for us.

How Can We Be Strong?

There are three ways we can be strong.

1. *Claim divine strength by faith.* We appropriate all these privileges and inheritances by faith. We can lose them or not enjoy them through fear. Fear is a dominant weapon of the devil.

We are encouraged to have a reverential fear of God our Father, but we must never be fearful.

Second Timothy 1:7 tells us that God has not given us the spirit of fear, but He has given us His power, love, and sound mind. We are expected to operate with a disciplined mind and to walk with wisdom and understanding.

The devil may throw fiery darts of fear, anxiety, worry, anger, jealousy, hopelessness, infirmities, bitterness, lust, deception, and so on against us. But he cannot defeat us if we understand how to exercise our faith and how to put on the whole armour of God.

The Bible declares that faith comes only by hearing the Word of God and the continued hearing of the Word of God (Romans 10:17). The Word of God is the source of our faith.

2. *Receive strength through prayer and praise.* Samson prayed to God to strengthen him while he was a prisoner of the Philistines. The Lord granted his request, and he killed more Philistines than he had ever done (Judges 16:5, 28).

We put on the armour through the skilful use of the Word. Every piece of the armour is put on through the declaration of the Word of God in faith and by prayer.

There are other ways we receive strength, and they are linked with prayer. These include praising God either in our natural language or in tongues (1 Corinthians 14:4, 13–15, 18, 39; Colossians 1:11; Nehemiah 8:10). The Bible says that if we pray in tongues, we edify ourselves, and we are strengthened—built up and fortified like an architectural edifice.

If we rejoice, we feel strong. Praising God is an antidote to sadness. If we put on the garment of praise by faith as the Lord has promised us, we overcome the spirit of heaviness.

3. *Receive and renew our strength when we wait on the Lord* (Isaiah 40:29–31):

> He giveth power to the faint; and to them that have no might he increaseth strength.
>
> Even the youths shall faint and be weary, and the young men shall utterly fall:
>
> But they that wait upon the Lord shall renew their strength; they shall mount up with wings as eagles; they shall run, and not be weary; and they shall walk, and not faint.

David did not defeat Goliath with Saul's armour. He refused to wear Saul's armour because he had never used it and was not skilful with it. Also, the armour of Saul was composed of human-made materials and based on the flesh.

David understood how to engage in battle because the battle of a righteous person is always the Lord's battle (1 Samuel 17:1–52). There is always a battle of words before an actual physical conflict takes place.

◊   Life is a battle of words and a conflict of thoughts.

The weapons of our warfare are not carnal. They are not human-made weapons like guns, arrows, swords, spears, tanks, missiles, and so on, for no matter how sophisticated they are, human-made weapons are no match for divine spiritual weapons.

Prayer, inclusive of praise, is the ultimate weapon and is more powerful than the latest human-made technological weapons. We rule and reign in this life through prayer. No matter the profession God has called you to, you maximise your potential through prayer.

David had experience in spiritual warfare. He had fought wild animals while taking care of the sheep. He understood how to battle with God's words and to neutralise demonic proclamations and curses.

Goliath said to David, "Do you think I am a dog that you have come to fight me with sticks?" and he cursed David by his gods. He challenged him and told him how the battle would end: "I will give your body to the birds and animals to eat" (1 Samuel 17:43–44).

His words were not empty words, casual and powerless. They were energised by his idols to harm David and to defeat him even before the battle took place.

◊ Our minds are battlegrounds. Words are not harmless. Death and life are in the power of the tongue.

David neutralised the demonically inspired words with God's words. Look at what he said in verses 45–47:

> Then said David to the Philistine, Thou comest to me with a sword, and with a spear, and with a shield: but I come to thee in the name of the Lord of hosts, the God of the armies of Israel, whom thou hast defied.

> This day will the Lord deliver thee into mine hand; and I will smite thee, and take thine head from thee; and I will give the carcases of the host of the Philistines this day unto the fowls of the air, and to the wild beasts of the earth; that all the earth may know that there is a God in Israel.

> And all this assembly shall know that the Lord saveth not with sword and spear: for the battle is the LORD'S, and he will give you into our hands.

The outcome of the battle was determined before the battle began.

Goliath had his gods, but David had Jehovah, the God of the heavens and the earth, Creator of the universe, omnipotent, omnipresent, and omniscient. Goliath represented the champion of the enemies of God's people (Satan), while David was in the typology of Christ, the champion of God's people.

The Lord has given us mighty weapons and His perfect armour which are activated by faith and the word of God.

CHAPTER 2

AUTHORITY AND POWER OVER THE ENEMY

Who is the enemy? We are at war, and the real enemy is Satan.

In the kingdom of darkness, Satan reigns supreme (Luke 4:5-8). He is the god of this world (2 Corinthians 4:4), the prince of this world (John 14:30), and the prince of the power of the air (Ephesians 2:1–3).

Satan, once called Lucifer, was an archangel whose pride and rebellion destroyed his position in heaven (Ezekiel 28:11–17; Isaiah 14:12–14). He was cast out of heaven with one-third of the angels (Revelation 12:4).

Satan has a very highly organized kingdom with various areas and levels of authority (Daniel 10:2–13, 20–21; Ephesians 6:10–18). It is a four-level hierarchy.

1. *Principalities* (Greek *archas*) are ruling demon spirits set over nations and regions of the earth and governments at the

national and continental levels, including international and intergovernmental agencies.

2. *Powers* (Greek *exousias*) are territorial demon spirits operating to exercise authority and power at different levels of government operations.

3. *Rulers of the darkness of this world* (*kosmokratoras*) are lords of the world and princes of this age responsible for the darkness and the blindness of the world at large.

4. *Spiritual wickedness in heavenly places* manifests as demon spirits working wickedness and bringing oppression, depression, possession, and affliction to people.

So, we can see that we are not fighting human beings.

Your enemies are not your neighbours, coworkers, in-laws, politicians, Christian leaders, or religious people and their religions. They may be tools and agents of these unseen enemies. The fruit is the evidence of the root.

Jesus spoke to the fig tree that no one would eat the fruit of the tree because it had leaves without any fruit. The story was told in Mark 11:12-21.

We read about the outcome of the words of Jesus in Mark 11:20:

And in the morning, as they passed by, they saw the fig tree dried up from the roots.

Jesus spoke to the tree and it dried up from the roots.

Take your fight to the root. We are often fighting at the level of what we can see, feel, taste, and touch; that is the fruit that is evident to the senses. Neutralise the root by the word of God and prayers, and the fruit will be no more.

We wrestle not against flesh and blood the scriptures say.

Weapons of the Enemy

These weapons include pride, lust, rebellion, deception, prayerlessness, fear, worry, anxiety, discouragement, unbelief, doubt, disobedience, anger and resentment, condemnation, guilt, self-pity, hatred, unforgiveness, envy and jealousy, strife and contention, violence, destruction, obsession, compulsion, depression, oppression, possession, infirmities, sickness and illnesses, ignorance, greed, cruelty, and murder.

There are demon spirits responsible for the operations of these weapons. These demon spirits are recognized by their manifestations.

Whenever you begin to see the operations of these demon spirits through their manifestations, you need to deploy your spiritual weapons—the armour of God—to neutralise them and render them ineffective and harmless against you or your loved ones.

Our Position and Authority in Christ

Satan has been totally defeated by Jesus Christ at Calvary through the cross. He defeated him on our behalf and not for himself (1 John 3:8; Hebrews 2:14–15; Colossians 2:13–15; Revelation 1:18).

Hebrews 2:14–15 tell us,

> Forasmuch then as the children are partakers of flesh and blood, he also himself likewise took part of the same; that through death he might destroy him that had the power of death, that is, the devil;

> And deliver them who through fear of death were all their lifetime subject to bondage.

Colossians 2: 14-15:

Blotting out the handwriting of ordinances that was against us, which was contrary to us, and took it out of the way, nailing it to his cross;

And having spoiled principalities and powers, he made a shew of them openly, triumphing over them in it.

◊ It is now our responsibility to enforce Calvary's victory and Satan's defeat.

Anyone who believes in Jesus Christ, repents of his or her sins, and confesses Him as Lord and Saviour becomes saved. These individuals become children of God, ambassadors of Christ, kings and priests in the kingdom of God, and are entitled to all the rights and privileges of the kingdom as heirs of God and joint heirs with Christ (John 1:12–13; Acts 2:21; John 3:3; Romans 8:14–17; 10:9–10, 13; Galatians 3:26, 29; 4:6–7; 1 Peter 2:5, 9; 2 Peter 1:3–4; Revelation 1:6; 5:10).

Galatians 4:7 reads:

Wherefore thou art no more a servant, but a son; and if a son, then an heir of God through Christ.

Jesus restored the dominion and authority which Adam lost through sin and disobedience (Genesis 1–3).

Our Adamic nature is dead, crucified with Christ (Romans 6:6–11), and we are a new creation in Christ (2 Corinthians 5:17).

This is what the Bible says in 2 Corinthians 5:17:

> Therefore if any man be in Christ, he is a new creature: old things are passed away; behold, all things are become new.

We are raised with Christ and enthroned with Him in heavenly places (Ephesians 2:4–6) far above all principalities and powers and might and dominion and every name that is named, not only in this age, but also in that which is to come (Ephesians 1:19–21).

Christ is in us; the hope of glory and our lives are hidden with Christ in God (Colossians 1:27; 2:9–12; 3:3; John 17:22). We are complete in Jesus Christ, who is the head over every ruler and authority.

This is what the Bible says about us:

> And of his fulness have all we received, and grace for
> grace. (John 1:16)

Apart from our legal position of authority in Christ, we have His indwelling power to make effective this authority in our daily Christian walks (Galatians 2:20; 1 John 4:3–4; 5:4–5; John 1:16; Ephesians 3:20; Luke 10:19). We have weapons of warfare that are not carnal (2 Corinthians 10:3–6; Ephesians 6:10–18).

We have authority over all the power of the enemy (Luke 10:19). Our enemies are Satan, principalities, powers, rulers of the darkness of this world, and spiritual wickedness in heavenly places (Ephesians 6:12; 1 Peter 5:8; James 4:7; Romans 16:20). We have authority as Christ's ambassadors (John 17:18; 2 Corinthians 5:20); as heirs and joint heirs (Romans 8:17; Galatians 3:29; 4:1–7); as sons, kings, and priests (John 1:12; Revelation 1:6; 5:10; 1 Peter 2:5, 9; Romans 5:17); and as soldiers of Christ (2 Timothy 2:3). We are called to reign on the earth as kings.

We exercise our authority by the spoken word in commands or decrees, and through all kinds of prayers.

CHAPTER 3

THE ARMOUR OF
A SOLDIER

The nature of the military in any country is to be ready for emergencies, having prepared adequately on a regular basis. They train with their weapons and achieve expertise in deploying them.

The Roman army consisted of the legions, auxiliaries, and other allied forces. Only a Roman citizen could become a member of the legion.

Paul, in the book of Ephesians, on observing a Roman soldier and his armour, tried to draw a parallel with the revelation he had received about the armour of God (Ephesians 6:13–18).

The armour of God is far more powerful than that of a Roman soldier and relevant throughout all generations. Its power is limitless because God is omnipotent.

Since a Christian is a soldier of Jesus Christ (2 Timothy 2:3), he has to be equipped with the armour of God in order to carry out his duties without being captured by the enemy.

The Roman army developed a wide variety of weapons and armour that were used during wars. Their arsenal was more than what was described by the apostle Paul. What armour the Roman soldier wore depended on his assignment.

Let us now examine the personal weapons of the Roman soldier and compare them with the armour of God in chapter 4.

PERSONAL WEAPONS OF THE ROMAN SOLDIER [1]

1. *Clothing, including a sword belt.* The Roman soldier wore a tunic made of wool under the armour. He wore a sword belt called the balteus. He wore a skirt of leather or fabric strips called the pteruges around his waist to protect his upper legs. The pteruges could be fitted with small metal studs and plates to provide additional protection. The belt protected the vital organs of reproduction, the kidneys, and the great vessels in the abdomen.

2. *Breastplate.* There were different types of breastplates used by the Roman soldier. One of such was called the Lorica segmentata. This was a type of body armour with breast- and backplates covering the front and the back.

It also had shoulder guards to protect the shoulders. Some troops wore segmental armour called the manica (armguard) on one or both arms. The breastplate protected the heart and the great vessels as well as the lungs. These are important organs in the body.

3. *Boots (Caligae).* These were military boots worn by legionaries and auxiliaries in the Roman Empire. They were made from leather and went up the centre of the foot and to the ankle. Iron hobnails were hammered into the sole for added strength. These made it impossible for the soldier to slip on any terrain while advancing or getting ready for battle. The iron hobnails could also become an offensive weapon in close combat. Sheet metal plates (greave) were worn to protect the legs.

4. *Shield.* There were different sizes of shields carried by the Roman soldier depending on his role at that particular time. Oval, circular, and rectangular shields were used throughout Roman history. The scutum type was a large shield but light enough to be carried in one hand. Its large height and width covered most of the soldier's body, protecting him from getting hit by missile fire and in hand-to-hand combat. The metal boss, or umbo, in the centre of the scutum also made it an auxiliary punching weapon. The implication of this is that the shield, while being a major defensive weapon, could be used as an offensive weapon in close-quarter combat.

The soldier might also carry half-dozen lead-weighted throwing darts, referred to as the plumbatae, clipped to the back of the shield. Again, we see that the shield was not only a defensive weapon.

5. *Helmet.* The helmets the soldiers wore varied over time. The objective was to cover the head, therefore protecting it. The helmets covered the back of the neck. Some were fitted with cheek guards.

6. *Sword.* (a) A pugio was a dagger used by Roman soldiers, about twenty centimetres in length, it was likely used as a sidearm and attached to the belt. (b) The gladius, which is Latin for sword, was a double-sided short sword, half a metre in length. (c) The spatha was a longer sword than the gladius.

7. *Heavy Artillery.* Other weapons, including spears, javelins, bows, and crossbows were used. Spears (hastae) and javelins were also used as offensive weapons. A haste (spear) was about 1.8 metres (6 feet) in length. A heavy javelin (pilum) was less than 2 metres long. Bows and crossbows are arrow-shooting weapons.

OLD TESTAMENT SCRIPTURES REFERRING TO NATURAL WEAPONS

There are scriptures in the Old Testament that mention the weapons used in warfare.

The weapons of Goliath (1 Samuel 17:4–7): helmet of brass, a coat of mail, greaves of brass upon his legs, a target of brass between his shoulders, a spear with an iron head, and someone carrying a heavy shield in front of him. He was fully equipped for war.

The weapons of Saul (1 Samuel 17:38–39): helmet of brass, coat of mail, and a sword.

The scriptures recognise these weapons (Jeremiah 46:3–4; 9; 51:11; Ezekiel 38:4; 39:3, 9). You can see all the weapons of war mentioned in these scriptures.

◊ The battle belongs to the Lord, and He has given us an armour.

The whole culture of the military of any nation is to prepare for war and unexpected emergencies. That is why they have drills and training exercises for different scenarios. They practice with their weapons using blank bullets. Whenever you see a well-armed soldier or anti-terrorist or anti-riot police officer, there is a vigilance in your spirit, or there is fear if you are about to do something wrong. You believe this person is trained to put you down and neutralise your threats even in the time of peace.

As believers, we should be trained in the use of our spiritual weapons. We should be sober, vigilant, and ready to disarm the enemy and neutralise his threats, even though he has been defeated by our commander in chief, our Lord Jesus Christ as shown in 1 Peter 5:8–9:

Be sober, be vigilant; because your adversary the devil, as a roaring lion, walketh about, seeking whom he may devour:

Whom resist stedfast in the faith, knowing that the same afflictions are accomplished in your brethren that are in the world.

Hallelujah!

We should be as skilful in the use of spiritual weapons as David was with his sling and stones (1 Samuel 16:18).

Be prepared before the battle starts against you.

Best wishes if you think that Christians don't have spiritual battles to fight.

CHAPTER 4

THE WHOLE ARMOUR OF GOD

Every believer should know that we are called to fight the good fight of faith. There is a fight, and we know that it is a good fight because our Lord Jesus Christ won the victory for us. He spoiled principalities and powers, triumphed over them, and now He sits as King of kings and Lord of lords at the right hand of God.

He gave us authority to tread upon serpents and scorpions (all demonic and evil spirits of any rank), and power over all the powers of the enemy. And He declared to us that nothing shall by any means hurt us (1 Timothy 6:12; Colossians 2:15; Ephesians 1:20–21; Luke 10:19).

He gave us a complete armour to guarantee our victory in spiritual warfare without becoming a casualty of war.

He is also training us for unexpected emergencies so that we can stand our ground and advance to conquer new territories.

We learn about God's perfect armour in Ephesians 6:10–18.

A PERFECT AND COMPLETE ARMOUR

There are seven pieces, or parts, of this armour. The number seven represents perfection in the scriptures. The whole armour of God is a perfect and complete armour, and that is why it is called the whole armour of God. The protection is total: front, back, sides, round and round; head and feet. God will never give us armour that is incomplete.

I struggled with this for a while because I thought there were only six pieces. Six stands for the number of humankind and their efforts.

The armour is for a heavenly human, not for a natural human. Though the description of the armour was patterned after the armour of a Roman soldier, it is effectively a spiritual armour relevant to every generation, and across continents, languages, and people who have accepted the Lord Jesus Christ as their Lord and Saviour.

It is for a people who are born again, redeemed by the blood of Jesus Christ, sanctified, justified, and completely regenerated as new individuals. It guarantees total victory over the strategies, devices, fiery darts, and weapons of the enemy.

These are not human-made weapons. They are activated by faith and the Word of God. All the weapons are interrelated in their functions.

> The whole armour of God is a perfect and complete armour.

The armour of God is activated by faith and the Word of God.

All the weapons are interrelated in their functions.

A Seven-Part Armour

1. Belt of Truth

As we read in chapter 3, the belt holds the sword and the dagger in position for effective deployment in combat. The belt also protects the vital organs and the ability to reproduce and be fruitful.

Without a solid foundation of the truth of the Word of God, we will not be able to make disciples of all nations. We will not be able to reproduce healthy children for the Lord.

The belt of truth guards us against the lies of the enemy. Jesus is the way, the truth, and the life (John 14:6). Jesus is not *a* truth or *one of* the ways revealing truth. Jesus Christ is *the* truth. As written in John 8:32:

And ye shall know the truth, and the truth shall make you free.

Jesus does not only set you free. He makes you free, liberating you from all bondages as you receive the revelation of who Jesus Christ is.

Satan cannot abide in the truth because there is no truth in him. The Bible calls him a liar and the father of lies. God is the God of truth (Psalm 31:5).

The Word of God is absolute truth and carries veracious authority (Galatians 1:8). Facts change, but the truth of the Word of God stands the test of time. It actually transcends time. Do not believe the lies of the devil. Believe the truth of God's words.

◊ Jesus Christ will come back again. That is absolute truth.

The Word of God was inspired by the Holy Spirit (2 Peter 1:21; 2 Timothy 3:16–17; Numbers 23:19), and He is the Spirit of truth (John 14:17; 15:26; 16:13; 1 John 5:6).

2. Breastplate of Righteousness

The breastplate of righteousness protects the vital spiritual organ— the heart. This is not the natural heart that you can feel beating. Christ, who knew no sin, was made sin for us so that those who accept His finished work at Calvary are made the righteousness of God in Christ (2 Corinthians 5:21).

We are the righteousness of God. Now we reign with Him, seated at the right hand of the Father, having received the gift of righteousness (Romans 5:17; 3:26).

Romans 5:17 reads:

For if by one man's offence death reigned by one; much more they which receive abundance of grace and of the gift of righteousness shall reign in life by one, Jesus Christ.

Now we are reigning with Him.

Righteousness means right standing with God. It is the right to live in the presence of the Father and the ability to stand before Him without condemnation, sin consciousness, guilt, or feelings of inferiority.

The Father always sees us in Jesus Christ, and we are accepted in the beloved. It is time to be sonship conscious.

Jesus put on righteousness as a breastplate (Isaiah 59:17), and righteousness was the belt of His loins (Isaiah 11:5). So, it is time we put on the breastplate of righteousness and walk in dominion over sin.

It is also the breastplate of faith and love (1 Thessalonians 5:8). The heart is the source of faith and love. In other words, faith and love emanate from the state of the heart.

The Bible says in Proverbs 4:23,

Keep thy heart with all diligence; for out of it are the issues of life

It also commands us to keep the words of God in our hearts (Proverbs 4:21).

◊ "Guard your heart" is a military command to protect it from all evil emotions.

You realise that nothing can separate us from the love of God (Romans 8:37–39). God loves us. What a powerful weapon against low self-esteem and feelings of unworthiness.

The Lord gives us the ability to love people, even our enemies. We receive the capacity to love when we put on the breastplate of love.

As the Roman soldier wore arm guards, believers are expected to put on the armour of righteousness on the right hand and on the left hand as shown in the Bible:

> By the word of truth, by the power of God, by the armour of righteousness on the right hand and on the left (2 Corinthians 6:7).

We preach the Word of God in righteousness, and the works of our hands provide the evidence of our righteousness.

3. *Sandals of the Readiness to Proclaim the Gospel of Peace*

The footwear of the Roman soldier revealed his readiness to engage swiftly in battle. The shoes gave him mobility. He was ready for sudden attacks and prepared to fight without worrying about tripping or falling.

Preparation is important if we are to succeed in any endeavour. When we are ready, we will not be caught unawares. We can preach in season and out of season.

Putting on the sandals of the gospel of peace implies our readiness to preach the gospel in every circumstance.

The gospel is preaching good news to the poor, healing the broken-hearted, preaching deliverance to the captives, praying for the recovery of sight to the blind, setting at liberty those who are bruised, and preaching the acceptable year of the Lord (Luke 4:18–19).

The Roman soldier wore iron hobnails on the soles of his shoes which can become an offensive weapon in close combat. They can also be used to spike snakes, scorpions, and other reptiles. In other words, the sandals, though majorly a defensive weapon, can be used for offensive warfare.

◊　The preaching of the gospel is a demonstration of power as captives are set free.

Putting on the sandals of the gospel of peace by confessing the Word of God prepares us to tread upon serpents and scorpions (demonic spirits) and to exercise power over all the power of the enemy. We have the promise that nothing shall by any means hurt us (Luke 10:19; Psalm 91:13) as we go about fulfilling our calling.

4.　Shield of Faith

Using the shield of faith, we quench all the fiery darts of the wicked one. We are commanded to take this shield.

The fiery darts may include the following: pride, lust, rebellion, deception, prayerlessness, fear, worry, anxiety, discouragement, unbelief, doubt, disobedience, anger and resentment, condemnation, guilt, self-pity, hatred, unforgiveness, envy and jealousy, strife and contention, destruction, obsession, compulsion, depression, oppression, possession, infirmities, sickness and illnesses, ignorance, greed; cruelty, violence, and murder.

When the enemy fires the darts of fear, anxiety, and worry, or any dart, take the shield of faith and quench that dart. You neutralise these darts with the Word of God.

Every piece of the armour is activated by the Word of God. Faith comes by hearing and hearing of the Word of God (Romans 10:17). If you believe, you will speak. Speak to the mountain, command it to be cast into the sea; command the destruction of the dart and issue decrees (Mark 11:22–24; Matthew 17:20).

Remember, the Lord is our shield and buckler (Psalms 3:3; 5:12; 18:2, 30).

When you confess the Word of God, your faith increases. The Word of God goes to your heart faster when your ears hear these words from your mouth than when you hear another person speak them.

Hebrews chapter 11 describes the people of faith in the Old Testament and how they defeated all that the devil threw at them.

The shield of faith is not only a defensive weapon. As shown in chapter 3, it can also be used as an offensive weapon in close-quarter combat. Ephesians chapter 6 tells us about wrestling against demonic forces. Wrestling is a close-quarter style of fighting.

5. Helmet of Salvation

This armour provides protection for the head. You must have an assurance of your security in Christ.

This helmet reminds us of the hope of salvation (1 Thessalonians 5:8). It provides protection for our minds, a defence against demonically inspired thoughts. We are saved from fear, anxiety, doubts, and worry.

God has not given us the spirit of fear but of power, love, and a sound mind (2 Timothy 1:7). The Bible says that we have the mind of Christ (1 Corinthians 2:16). Christ has been made unto us wisdom and knowledge, and, therefore, wisdom is available to us for whatever God assigns to us.

Since our mind is the battleground, we need all the resources that the Lord has provided for us.

Though we walk in the flesh as physical human beings, we do not war after the flesh; for the weapons of our warfare are not human-made carnal weapons but mighty through God-given spiritual weapons for pulling down strongholds of sickness, poverty, failure, unbelief, false ideologies, fear, and death.

We cast down all imaginations emanating from the evil one. And we cast down every high thing (doctrines and philosophies of humans) that exalts itself against the knowledge of God. We bring into captivity every thought contrary to the will and purpose of God to the obedience of Christ (2 Corinthians 10:3–6).

The will of God is that we prosper and be in health (3 John:2). Our minds are for meditation, not worry. The principles for meditation and worry are the same, though the scriptures encourage the former and discourage the latter. Take thoughts of worry captive, and replace them with the Word of God.

Meditate only about whatever is true, honest, just, pure, lovely, of good report, of virtue, and praiseworthy (Philippians 4:8).

6. Sword of the Spirit

Take the sword of the Spirit, which is the Word of God, and wage offensive warfare with it.

You overcome Satan, principalities, powers, rulers of the darkness of this world and spiritual wickedness in heavenly places by the blood of Jesus and the Word of God (Revelation 12:11).

You declare the Lordship of Jesus Christ over your life, family, work, ministry, and all the realms of operations in the nations of the world that the Lord has assigned to you.

Declare your redemption by the blood of Jesus, and claim all the redemptive blessings provided for us as joint heirs with Christ and as heirs of God through the shed blood of Jesus.

This is when you begin to do praise warfare. Put the high praises of God in your mouth; declare the prophetic words and the rhema God gave you in that specific season (Psalm 149:1–9). Remember that praise is an aspect of worship, and you can dance, clap, shout, laugh and play musical instruments if you can.

When you are confessing scriptures, you are waging warfare with the sword of the Spirit. It is the most offensive weapon we have.

Revelation 19:13 describes His name as "The Word of God":

> And he was clothed with a vesture dipped in blood: and his name is called The Word of God

In Revelation 19:15 The Lord Jesus Christ was revealed as having a sharp sword going out of His mouth with which He would smite the nations during his second coming.

This sharp sword is the rhema word that will be spoken by the Lord.

Confess the psalms, especially Psalms 91, 23, 27, and 121. Use the sword of the Spirit skilfully.

Confess the first part of Isaiah 49:2: "And he has made my mouth like a sharp sword."

Use your mouth to declare God's words in Isaiah, Jeremiah, the Gospels, and the Epistles, declaring your redemptive blessings of peace, salvation, sanctification, healing, health, guidance, victory, prosperity, and His presence.

Death and life are in the power of the tongue, and they who love it shall eat the fruit thereof (Proverbs 18:21). Know the verses of scripture that guarantee your victory. Jesus defeated the devil by speaking the Word of God (Luke 4:1–11).

7. Watching and Praying with All Prayers and Supplication in the Spirit for All the Saints

I believe this represents the heavy artillery of the Roman army or any modern army. This is the equivalence of non-close-contact warfare with heavy armoury and includes other weapons, such as spears, javelins, bow, and crossbows. In the modern army, it includes armoured tanks, missiles, and drones.

It incorporates all types of prayers, including thanksgiving, praise, worship, praying and singing in your heavenly language (tongues), petition, supplication, intercession, groans and travails, consecration and dedication, repentance and confession of sin, corporate prayer, prayer of importunity, prayer of faith, prayer of agreement, prophetic prayers and actions, decrees, silent prayers, and conversational prayers (Ephesians 3:20; 6:18–19; 2 Corinthians 10:3–6; Psalm 149:1–9; Ezekiel 37:1–10; 1 Peter 5:8–9; James 4:7; 5:14–15; Matthew 16:19; 18:18–20; 21:22; Mark 11:24, 1 Corinthians 14:2; Romans 8:26; Luke 11:1, 5–13; Acts 4:23–31, and many of the psalms).

By prayer we bring to pass His will on the earth as it is in heaven. We enforce His will and implement His decisions.

You pray without ceasing day and night. And as the Lord leads, you shift from one mode of prayer to another. Remember that praise is a component of prayer.

Every Piece of the Armour Can Be Used for Defence and for Offence

Every piece of the armour can be used for defence and for offence in spiritual battle.

Some are majorly defensive weapons (1–5) but can be used as offensive weapons in prayer warfare. Others are primarily offensive weapons (6 and 7), but they can be used for defence too. The Roman soldier, as used by Paul in the illustration of the armour, did not only use his sword as an offensive weapon but had spears, daggers, darts, javelins, bows, and crossbows.

Every weapon is made effective by speech and made operational by the Word of God which is living and powerful and sharper than a two-edged sword (Hebrews 4:12). The Word of God is fire (Jeremiah 5:14; 20:9; 23:28–29), and like a hammer (Jeremiah 23:29).

Putting on the whole armour of God prepares a believer for whatever comes against him. He is ready to stand his ground in the evil day and the not so evil day. It is not wise to engage in spiritual warfare without putting on the armour of God.

Other Weapons and Resources Available to Us

There are other weapons and resources available to a believer in spiritual battle. These weapons are incorporated into the seventh piece of the armour as described earlier.

They include:

1. Praise warfare (Psalms 8:2; 149:6–9)

2. The blood of Jesus (Revelation 12:11; Exodus 12:12–13)

3. The name of Jesus (Mark 16:17–18; Philippians 2:9–11)

4. The fruit of the Spirit (Holiness) (Galatians 5:22–23; John 14:30; 1 Corinthians 13:4–8)

5. The anointing and the gifts of the Holy Spirit (1 Corinthians 12:1–11)

6. Warrior angels. Angels are our ministering spirits, and they are part of God's army. They assist us in spiritual battle (Psalm 34:7; 2 Kings 6:16–17).

7. Fasting (Matthew 17:21; Isaiah 58:6)

8. Holy Communion (1 Corinthians 11:23–26)

CHAPTER 5

THE PRACTICAL WAY TO PUT ON THE WHOLE ARMOUR OF GOD

LEVEL 1

Level 1 is when you are pressed for time. For example, professionals such as doctors, nurses, pharmacists and other health workers, administrators, soldiers, police officers, politicians (ministers, governors, chairmen of parastatals, and so on), ministers of the gospel (apostles, prophets, evangelists, pastors, and teachers). Or if you are a Christian brother or sister and for whatever reason you are pressed for time and sense or hear the Holy Spirit warning you of a demonic presence or activity, you can put on the whole armour of God instantaneously. You declare, "I put on the whole armour of God right now in the name of the Lord Jesus Christ. Amen." If you cannot declare out loud, say it under your breath.

After this, if the Lord reveals the nature of the demonic presence or activity, you can pray specifically and use your authority to bind and cast it out. But if it is not revealed, begin to pray in the Holy Spirit (in tongues, your heavenly language), and plead the blood of Jesus.

LEVEL 2

If you have more time than described above but cannot spend a long time to pray and confess the Word of God, you can be more specific as you put on the whole armour of God. Put on the whole armour of God as follows:

Belt of Truth

"I gird my loins with the belt of truth," or, "I fasten on the belt of truth."

Breastplate of Righteousness

"I put on the breastplate of righteousness, the breastplate of faith and love" (1 Thessalonians 5:8), and, "I put on the armour of righteousness on the right hand and on the left" (2 Corinthians 6:7).

Shoes (Sandals) of the Readiness of the Gospel of Peace

"I put on my feet shoes of the readiness of the gospel of peace," or, "I put on sandals of the readiness to proclaim the gospel of peace."

Shield of Faith

I take the shield of faith by which I am able to quench all the fiery darts of the wicked.

Helmet of Salvation

I put on the helmet of salvation; the helmet of the hope of salvation (1 Thessalonians 5:8).

Sword of the Spirit

I take the sword of the Spirit, which is the Word of God.

Praying at All Times in the Spirit

I pray this day, at all times, in the Spirit, praying always with all prayer and supplication. I will keep alert, watching with all perseverance, making supplication for all the saints.

Once you understand how to put on the armour as described, you can use your own language and modify how you make these declarations. Think about the dressing of a Roman soldier. You can do this as you prepare for work or during your quiet time. Putting on the armour prepares you for the day. And you definitely won't be a casualty as you minister during your daily activities.

Continue to pray throughout the day in your language and in tongues, and as the Lord directs you.

LEVEL 3

Whenever you are going to minister under nonemergency situations, you will need to spend more time in prayer as you put on the armour of God. This involves a lot of confession of the Word of God in prayer. When you enter enemy territory, you will operate without fear.

This is not a doctrine. You may or may not choose to do it this way. The Lord taught me to do it this way, and it has been working for me. I have taught these concepts of how to put on the armour of God to many churches and at ministers' conferences as well as prayer meetings. I have taught this one-on-one with believers. I don't go out to minister, especially in unknown settings, without spending time in prayer and putting on the armour of God.

It is possible to make these confessions without specifically declaring that you are putting on each piece of the armour. You can also confess other scriptures as the Lord reveals them to you.

◊ Death and life are in the power of the tongue.

Put on the whole armour of God with declarations as follows.

> As I begin to make these confessions in prayer, I become continually stronger in the Lord and in the power of His might. As I obey His command to put on the armour, I receive by faith all blessings associated with this obedience in the mighty name of Jesus Christ. Amen.

Belt of Truth

I gird my loins with the belt of truth. Jesus is the Way, the Truth, and the Life (John 14:6); therefore, I know the way and I will never be lost or confused this day in the name of Jesus. I will not be a victim of deception, seduction and dullness of mind.

According to Colossians 1:9–10: In the name of Jesus I am filled with the knowledge of God's will in all wisdom and spiritual understanding. I walk worthy of the Lord, fully pleasing Him today and I shall be fruitful in every good work and I am increasing in all the knowledge of God.

The Lord will instruct me in the way that I shall go and He will guide me with His eye (Psalm 32:8).

According to Psalm 25: 4, Lord, show me Your ways and teach me Your paths.

Lord, You are the truth, and the Holy Spirit is the Spirit of truth. Help me to speak the word of truth today as Your Word is truth. I resist all lying spirits and forbid them from operating against me and the ministry You have given me today. I know the truth, and this truth makes me free. The Son of God has made me free, and I am free indeed.

As I declare Your words, let them be spirit and life. I have the life of God in me. The Bible says that He who has the Son has life (1 John 5:12).

The law of the Spirit of life in Christ Jesus has made me free from the law of sin and death (Romans 8:2) and terminates the operations of the law of death working through any infirmity in my body. I curse any hidden sickness to wither and die from its roots like the fig tree. Hallelujah. I declare that I shall not die but live to declare the works of the Lord (Psalm 118:17).

According to Psalm 91:16, I declare that with long life the Lord will satisfy me, and He will show me His salvation. Amen. The Lord will bless my bread and my water according to Exodus 23, verses 25 and 26. He will take sickness away from me, and the number of my days He will fulfil.

I am wonderfully and marvellously created. I demand in the name of Jesus Christ that every cell, tissue, organ, and system in my body perform a perfect work and conform to the will and purpose of almighty God, my Father for my life. I command my body not to cooperate with the enemy to bring disease and afflictions to me in the mighty name of Jesus Christ, my Lord and Saviour. Amen.

I charge my body by the power of the Holy Spirit and in the name of the Lord Jesus Christ and by the power and the authority of His holy Word to be healed and made whole.

Breastplate of Righteousness

I put on the breastplate of righteousness. I put on the breastplate of faith and love and the armour of righteousness on the right hand and on the left hand.

I am the righteousness of God in Christ Jesus.

Whatever I lay my hands on shall prosper. Whatever I bind on earth is bound in heaven, and whatever I loose on earth is loosed in heaven. Because I believe in the name of the Lord Jesus Christ, these signs shall follow me according to Mark 16:17. I will cast out demons, speak with new tongues, and will be immune to all serpents, natural or spiritual, and to all poisons in drink or food. They shall not hurt me.

I claim total immunity to all poisons in whatever form, natural or spiritual. I shall lay hands on the sick, and they shall recover in the name of Jesus. Amen.

This day I will not walk according to the counsel of the ungodly, nor stand in the path of sinners, nor sit in the seat of the scornful. My delight shall be in the law of the Lord, and on these I shall meditate day and night.

I am like a tree that is planted by the rivers of water that brings forth its fruit in its season, whose leaf does not wither, and in whatever I do I shall prosper (Psalm 1:1–3).

I am a child of God; I overcome and defeat this evil world through my faith, and I believe that Jesus Christ is the Son of God (1 John 5:4–5). I shall walk and live by faith today, and I will not be ruled by my natural senses (Galatians 3:11; 2 Corinthians 5:7).

My heart is filled with love by the Holy Spirit today (Romans 5:5), and therefore, I will walk in love and forgiveness throughout this day by the power of the Holy Spirit and allow my faith to operate by this love of God (1 Corinthians 13).

CHAPTER 6

THE REST OF THE ARMOUR

The following are the remaining aspects of the armour.

Shoes of the Readiness of the Gospel of Peace

I put on the shoes of the gospel of peace.

As I preach the gospel, the Lord will confirm the Word of God with signs and wonders. According to Luke 10:19, I have the authority and the power to tread upon serpents and scorpions (all demonic agents) and over all the powers of the enemy, and nothing shall by any means hurt me.

I shall tread upon the lion and the adder; the young lion and the dragon shall I trample under my feet in the name of Jesus (Psalm 91:13).

The Spirit of the Lord is upon me because He has anointed me to preach the gospel to the poor. He has sent me to heal the broken-hearted, to preach deliverance to the captives and recovery of sight to the blind, to set at liberty those who are bruised, and to preach the acceptable year of the Lord (Luke 4:18–19).

As I preach the gospel, the God of peace shall bruise Satan under my feet shortly (Romans 16:20).

The Lord will instruct me in the way that I shall go, and He will guide me with His eye (Psalm 32:8).

Shield of Faith

I take the shield of faith by which I quench all the fiery darts of the wicked against me, my family, work, and ministry.

No weapon fashioned against me, my family, my ministry, and my work shall prosper. Every tongue that rises up against me and all that belongs to me in judgement I condemn in the name of the Lord Jesus Christ. Amen. This is my heritage in the Lord, and my righteousness is of the Lord (Isaiah 54:17).

Any counsel taken against me shall come to nothing, and any demonically inspired word spoken against me shall not stand for God is with me (Isaiah 8:9–10). If God be for me, who can be against me (Romans 8:31).

The Lord is with me as a mighty awesome one; therefore, my persecutors shall stumble, they shall not prevail; they shall be greatly ashamed for they shall not prosper. Their everlasting confusion will never come to an end (Jeremiah 20:11).

With the shield of faith, I destroy all the fiery darts of fear, anxiety, worry, anger, jealousy, pride, shame, racism, hopelessness, infirmities, bitterness, lust, deception, and all darts designed to steal, kill, and destroy. I render them totally powerless and ineffective in the name of the Lord Jesus Christ. Amen and Amen.

Helmet of Salvation

I put on the helmet of salvation, the helmet of the hope of salvation. God has not given me the spirit of fear but of power, love, and a sound mind (2 Timothy 1:7).

I have no fear, and I am filled with power, love, and a sound mind. I have the mind of Christ (1 Corinthians 2:16). Christ has been made unto me wisdom and knowledge, and therefore wisdom is available to me for whatever God assigns to me today. I am complete in Him, and I rule with Him over all principalities and powers (Colossians 2:3, 10, 15).

Though I walk in the flesh as a human being, I do not war after the flesh. For the weapons of my warfare are not human-made carnal weapons but mighty through God given spiritual weapons for pulling down strongholds of sickness, poverty, failure, unbelief, false ideologies, fear, and death in all who I shall minister to this day.

I cast down all imaginations emanating from the evil one, and I cast down every high thing (doctrines and philosophies of humans) that exalts itself against the knowledge of God. I bring into captivity every thought contrary to the will and purpose of God for my life to the obedience of Christ (2 Corinthians 10:3–6). The will of God is that I prosper and be in health (3 John: 2).

Sword of the Spirit

I take the sword of the Spirit, which is the Word of God.

The following are some of the confessions you can make. But remember that the Lord will give you a specific rhema word for specific situations during the day. The sword of the Spirit is the rhema word God gives you out of the abundance of the logos in your heart.

The following confessions are examples that have blessed many people. They do not constitute a prayer or confession manual that you must read in a dogmatic sense.

The most important thing is to memorise these scriptures and meditate as well as confess them till they are deposited in your heart. When the need arises, the Holy Spirit brings to your mind through your spirit a specific scripture, a rhema word, you need for a specific battle. These confessions centre around the redemptive blessings that the Lord provided for us through the blood of Jesus Christ.

These confessions are examples only. You can form your own confessions of scriptures. Remember that the pieces of the armour are voice activated.

I overcome Satan, principalities, powers, rulers of the darkness of this world, and spiritual wickedness in heavenly places by the blood of Jesus and the Word of God. I declare Jesus Christ as the Lord of my life.

I am redeemed by the blood of Jesus. I claim all the redemptive blessings provided for me as a joint heir with Christ and an heir of God through the shed blood of Jesus.

> I thank You, Lord, for You are my Jehovah Shalom—
> the Lord my peace.
>
> I thank You, Lord, for You are my Jehovah Nissi—the
> Lord my banner.

I thank You, Lord, for You are my Jehovah Rapha—
the Lord my healer.

I thank You, Lord, for You are my Jehovah Ra-ah—
the Lord my shepherd.

I thank You, Lord, for You are my Jehovah
Shammah—the Lord who is there.

I thank You, Lord, for You are my Jehovah Tsidkenu—
the Lord my righteousness.

I thank You, Lord, for You are my Jehovah Sabaoth—
the Lord of Hosts.

Father, according to Your Word in Romans 8:2, the
law of the Spirit of life in Christ Jesus makes me free
from the law of sin and death. Therefore, in the name
of Jesus Christ, my Lord and Saviour, I terminate
the operations of the law of death working sickness
in my body by the law of the spirit of life in Christ
Jesus. Amen!

According to Colossians 1:9–10, in the name of Jesus
I am filled with the knowledge of God's will in all
wisdom and spiritual understanding. I walk worthy
of the Lord, fully pleasing Him. I am fruitful in every
good work, and I am increasing in all the knowledge
of God.

I shall not die but live to declare the works of the Lord. (Psalm 118:17)

I give thanks to the Father who has qualified me to be a partaker of the inheritance of the saints in the light. (Colossians 1:11–12)

My inheritance includes health, healing, vigour, long life, success, prosperity (financially, materially, spiritually, physically, intellectually), victory, divine guidance, peace, righteousness, holiness, divine favour, grace, and strength. I am long lived, fruitful, healthy, durable, joyful, strong, full of peace, and joy in Jesus mighty name. (Colossians 1:11–12)

My Father in heaven has delivered me from the power of darkness and conveyed me into the kingdom of Christ, the Son of His love (Colossians 1:13). I am redeemed through the blood of Christ and forgiven all my sins. (Colossians 1:14)

Darkness has no more power over my life. I am the light of the world and the salt of the earth (Matthew 5:13–16). My light is shining so brightly before people revealing good works and God, my Father in heaven, is glorified.

I have power to tread upon serpents and scorpions (all demonic spirits and agents) and over all the power of the enemy, and nothing shall by any means hurt me. (Luke 10:19)

I have power to tread upon the lion and the adder; the young lion and the dragon (serpent) shall I trample underfoot in Jesus name. Amen.

> I dwell in the secret place of the Most High (El-Elyon), and I abide in the shadow of the Almighty (El-Shaddai). The Lord is my refuge and my fortress my God in whom I will trust. Surely, He shall deliver me from the snare of the fowler and from the noisome (perilous) pestilence. I shall not be afraid of the terror by night nor of the arrow that flies by day, nor of the pestilence that walks in darkness, nor of the destruction that lays waste at noon day. No evil shall befall me. No plague shall come near my dwelling place. The angels of the Lord are assigned to protect me. With long life the Lord will satisfy me, and He will continually show me His salvation (deliverance, healing, peace, and prosperity). (Psalm 91:1–16)

I am wonderfully and marvellously created. I demand in the name of Jesus Christ that every cell, tissue, organ, and system in my body perform a perfect work and conform to the will and purpose of almighty God, my Father for my life. I command my body not to cooperate with the enemy to bring disease and afflictions to me in the mighty name of Jesus Christ, my Lord and Saviour. Amen.

I charge my body by the power of the Holy Spirit and in the name of the Lord Jesus Christ, and by the power and the authority of His holy Word to be healed and made whole (Proverbs 12:18). Amen. Hallelujah.

According to Isaiah 53:5, I declare that He was wounded for my transgressions, He was bruised for my iniquities, the chastisement for my peace was upon Him and by His stripes I am healed. Amen.

According to Matthew 8:17, I declare that He took my infirmities And bore my sicknesses, and because Jesus took my infirmities and sicknesses upon His body on the cross two thousand years ago, I have no need to bear them again, and therefore I refuse to accept disease, sickness, and infirmities in my body in the name of Jesus Christ. Amen.

According to Psalm 23:4, I declare that though I walk through the valley of the shadow of death, I will fear no evil for the Lord is with me, His rod and staff comfort me.

According to God's promise in Jeremiah 30:17, the Lord will restore health to me and heal me of my wounds in Jesus name. Amen. Heal me, o Lord and I shall be healed; save me, and I shall be saved, for You are my praise (Jeremiah 17:14).

I will bless the Lord who forgives all my iniquities and heals all my diseases; who redeems my life from destruction and crowns me with loving kindness and tender mercies; who satisfies my mouth with good things and renews my youth like that of the eagle. (Psalm 103:1–5)

Let it be forever settled and established: it is God's will to heal me. I have a right to healing as well as forgiveness because I believe.

According to Galatians 3:13, 14, Christ has redeemed me from the curse of the law having become a curse for me. I have been redeemed from the curse of sickness, poverty, premature death, and blessed with the blessing of Abraham, including health, vigour, long life, material and spiritual prosperity, victory over all my enemies, and friendship with God.

Thank You, Father, that I am redeemed from sin and sickness. Thank You for deliverance both for soul and body. I believe it and praise You for it.

According to Psalm 107:20, He sent His Word and healed me and delivered me from all my destructions. The Lord is Jehovah Rapha—the Lord my healer. (Exodus 15:26)

According to Exodus 23:25, 26b, since I am serving the Lord my God, the Lord will bless my bread and my water. He will take away sickness from me, He will fulfil the number of my days.

According to Romans 8:11, the spirit of He who raised Jesus from the dead will also give life to my mortal body through His Spirit, who dwells in me. My body is therefore quickened, reinvigorated, made vibrant and whole in the name of Jesus Christ, my Lord and Saviour. Amen.

According to John 14:13, Whatsoever I ask in His name that He will do, so that the Father will be glorified in Jesus.

John 16:23-24 says,

> And in that day ye shall ask me nothing. Verily, verily, I say unto you, whatsoever ye shall ask the Father in my name, he will give it you.

> Hitherto have ye asked nothing in my name: ask, and ye shall receive, that your joy may be full.

According to the above scriptures, I ask the Father in the mighty name of Jesus Christ to grant to me good health, prosperity, success, and favour as I carry out my duties, and I believe I receive my answer by faith according to this word. Amen.

According to 1Peter 2:24:

> Who his own self bare our sins in his own body on the tree, that we, being dead to sins, should live unto righteousness: by whose stripes ye were healed.

According to this scripture, by His stripes I was healed over two thousand years ago. If I was healed then, I am healed now.

Confess Psalm 27:1

> The Lord is my light and my salvation; whom shall, I fear? The Lord is the strength of my life; of whom shall I be afraid?

According to 2 Timothy 1:7, God has not given me the spirit of fear but of power and of love and of a sound mind. I am strong in the Lord and in the power of His might.

CHAPTER 7

THE FINAL PIECE: PRAYING AT ALL TIMES IN THE SPIRIT

I pray this day, at all times in the Spirit, praying always with all prayer and supplication. I will keep alert, watching with all perseverance, making supplication for all the saints.

Holy Spirit, I pray that You will prompt me to pray in my heavenly language for people and nations on Your heart today.

Help me, O Lord, to pray for peace in all the troubled nations of the world, where there is war or famine or pestilence or natural disasters.

Help me to pray for my nation and the rulers so that there will be peace in my country. Help me to pray for the peace of Jerusalem and the Middle East.

Help me to pray for my family and friends: my spouse, children, grandchildren, brothers, sisters, parents, uncles, aunts for their welfare, protection, prosperity, and to pray for the salvation of those who are yet to know the Lord Jesus Christ as their Saviour.

Help me to pray for my ministry, all the churches and ministries that I am affiliated with and the ministers who You desire that I should pray for today and as You direct me.

Help me to pray for the ministry that You have for me today, that my service will fulfil Your plans and purposes.

Lord, prompt me to pray as the need arises throughout this day in line with Your purpose and desire.

Throughout this day and night, help me to pray without ceasing. I trust you, Holy Spirit, to give me promptings. I ask You, Lord, to put names of people in my heart to pray for and to lead me to pray for the places I go to. At all occasions enable me to pray in tongues under my breath.

As I mention nations, people, and people groups and situations to the Lord, please enable me to pray for them in my heavenly language. Throughout this day help me to sing in the Spirit also.

Help me to pray all types of prayers with the Spirit and with understanding, including thanksgiving, praise, worship, praying and singing in my heavenly language (tongues), petition, supplication, intercession, groans and travails, consecration and dedication, repentance and confession of sin, corporate prayer, prayer of importunity, prayer of faith, prayer of agreement, prophetic prayers and actions, decrees, silent prayer and conversational prayers (Ephesians 3:20; 6:18–19; 2 Corinthians 10:3–6; Psalm 149:1–9; Ezekiel 37:1–10; 1 Peter 5:8–9; James 4:7; 5:14–15; Matthew 16:19; 18:18–20; 21:22; Mark 11:24; 1 Corinthians 14:2; Romans 8:26; Luke 11:1, 5–13; Acts 4:23–31) and many of the psalms.

Lead me to pray with other brethren in agreement as You direct.

CHAPTER 8

CONCLUSION

Proverbs 12:6, 18 declares,

> The words of the wicked are to lie in wait for blood:
> but the mouth of the upright shall deliver them.
>
> There is that speaketh like the piercings of a sword:
> but the tongue of the wise is health.

The Bible declares that humans shall not live by bread alone but by every word that proceeds out of the mouth of God (Matthew 4:4). Jesus won every battle by the Word of God.

The Word of God is important to the believer. We must study, memorise, and meditate on the Word till the truth is planted fully in our hearts.

Out of the abundance of the logos of the Word of God in our hearts, the Holy Spirit can bring out a rhema word that is specific and powerful enough to neutralise and destroy the weapon of the enemy at that specific time.

The mind and the heart are the battlegrounds. The enemy attacks through our thoughts, belief systems, and imaginations. He may activate patterns of behaviour. We win the battle by being prepared, clothed with the armour of God.

Throughout the day and night, pray without ceasing as you are prompted by the Holy Spirit. The Lord will put names of people in your heart. You will go places and feel a prompting to pray. On all occasions pray in tongues under your breath without moving your lips.

You can mention nations, people, people groups, and situations to the Lord, and ask Him to enable you to pray for them in your heavenly language. You can sing in the Spirit also.

It is now our responsibility to enforce Calvary's victory and Satan's defeat. We put on the armour through the skilful use of the Word. Every piece of the armour is put on through the declaration of the Word of God in faith and by prayer.

Notes

1   Wikipedia: "Roman military personal equipment," last modified 16th November, 2020. https://en.wikipedia.org/wiki/Roman_military_personal_equipment.

PRAYER OF SALVATION

If you have not accepted the Lord Jesus Christ as your personal saviour, please pray this simple prayer and accept Him as your Lord and Saviour. Pray sincerely and accept Him wholeheartedly.

> Lord, I believe in my heart that Jesus Christ is the Son of God. I believe that I am a sinner and that Jesus Christ died on the cross to pay the penalty for my sins and to set me free. I believe that God raised Jesus from the dead for my justification.

> Father, I confess my sins and repent of them right now. I ask that You cleanse me with the blood of Jesus and make me a new creation. I confess and declare with my mouth that Jesus Christ is now my Lord and Saviour. Thank You, Lord, for saving me, and praise God, I am born again.